Read Well™

Down by the Sea

Copyright 2003 by Marilyn Sprick. All rights reserved.

Read Well and the Read Well logo are registered trademarks
of Sopris West Educational Services

08 07 06 05 04 03   6 5 4 3 2 1

Edited by Lisa Howard and Sandra L. Knauke
Cover design by Sue Campbell
Production assistance by Maria Coccaro

No portion of this work may be reproduced or transmitted
in any form or by any means, electronic or mechanical,
including photocopying or recording, or by any information
storage and retrieval system, without the express written
permission of the publisher.

ISBN 1-57035-663-7

Printed in China

Published and Distributed by

SOPRIS WEST
EDUCATIONAL SERVICES

4093 Specialty Place • Longmont, CO 80504 • (303) 651-2829
www.sopriswest.com

Down by the Sea

Book 8

UNITS 22 • 23 • 24

Read Well

Sopris West Educational Services

Theme
Down by the Sea

Celebrate the sea. Meet kindhearted Lobster Lou and Grandmother Octopus from the Jellyfish Hotel. Then travel to the big island of Hawaii and hear the story of Malia and her grandmother.

UNIT 22 • **Lobster's Lesson**

The Lobster Cafe 2
Fiction • Imaginative: By Marilyn Sprick, illustrated by Steve Clark
Summary: Visit crusty old Lobster Lou and learn why his friends throw him a surprise party.
Special Interactive Reading Activity: Lobster Lou's antennae twitch when he's thinking of helping someone else. During story reading, students use their hands as antennae to show when Lobster Lou is thinking of helping someone else.

Introduction 4

Chapter 1. Acts of Kindness 5

Chapter 2. Returning Some Kindness 14
Story Summary (Oral Retell) 27
Related Follow-up Activities: Pocket Chart Retell; Bookmaking

Related Literature

UNIT 23 • **Octopus Tales and Tentacles**

Story 1 • From the Library of the Jellyfish Hotel 30
Fiction • Imaginative: By Barbara Gunn and Marilyn Sprick, illustrated by Steve Clark
Summary: Remember kindly Lobster Lou? Return to the Jellyfish Hotel and meet another one of the hotel's many colorful residents—wise old Grandmother Octopus.
Special Interactive Reading Activity: During story reading, students sing and count along with Grandmother Octopus.
Story Summary (Oral Retell) 40

Unit 23 (continued)

Story 2 • How Lucky to Be an Octopus 42

Fiction • With Factual Information: By Marilyn Sprick, illustrated by Steve Clark

Summary: The little octopuses play a guessing game to find out what makes them so special.

Special Interactive Reading Activity: During story reading, students play a guessing game.

Related Follow-up Activity: Bookmaking

Related Literature

UNIT 24 • **Living by the Sea**

Story 1 • Malia at the Beach 59

Fiction • Realistic Narrative: By Marilyn Sprick and Barbara Gunn, illustrated by Susan Jerde

Summary: Malia celebrates her 7th birthday on the beach with her aunties, uncles, cousins, and her beloved grandmother.

Special Interactive Reading Activity: During story reading, students sing and play Malia's counting games.

Story 2 • Malia's Quilt 71

Fiction • Realistic Narrative: By Marilyn Sprick and Barbara Gunn, illustrated by Susan Jerde

Summary: Malia's grandmother comes to live with Malia and her parents and makes a very special gift for Malia.

Special Interactive Reading Activity: During story reading, students sing another of Malia's counting songs.

Related Follow-up Activity: Pocket Chart Retell; Bookmaking

Related Literature

Authors 85

Illustrators 86

UNIT 22

Lobster's Lesson

The Lobster Cafe

Chapter 1 • Acts of Kindness

Chapter 2 • Returning Some Kindness

STORY INTRODUCTION

Today's story is called *The Lobster Cafe*.

Everyone, what is the title of the story? (*The Lobster Cafe*)

This made-up story about a lobster and other sea creatures takes place deep at the bottom of the sea.

Marilyn Sprick wrote the story. She is the . . . (author).

The illustrator is Steve Clark.

The Lobster Cafe

by Marilyn Sprick

Illustrated by Steve Clark

Introduction

Resting deep at the bottom of the sea is an old ship known as the Jellyfish Hotel.

The Jellyfish Hotel is a splendid place with something for everyone—both young and old alike.

Chapter 1
Acts of Kindness

One of the most popular spots in the Jellyfish Hotel was the Lobster Cafe. The owner was a lobster named Lobster Lou. Lou was old and gruff. He sounded mean, but everyone knew that when Lou's antennae began twitching, it meant he was thinking about helping someone.

Everyone, who is the story about? (Lobster Lou)
Whenever Lou's antennae began twitching, it meant he was thinking about helping someone.
Put your arms in the air and pretend they are your antennae. Make them twitch.
Now put them down.

When Edith Eel first arrived at the Lobster Cafe, she was hungry and looking for a job. She didn't look very friendly, but Lou's antennae began twitching. Lou could tell Edith just needed a little kindness.

Whenever Lou's antennae began twitching, it meant he was thinking about helping someone.
Put your arms in the air and pretend they are your antennae. Make them twitch.
Now put your antennae down.
What do you think Lou was thinking about? (Helping Edith Eel)

Lou offered Edith Eel a job as a waitress. Soon Edith's sad and sort of scary look changed. She began pulling her teeth in and smiling a bit. Then she began chatting with the guests, and before long she was making friends.

The cafe customers came to love Edith. From the kitchen, Lou watched happily. When all the cooking and cleaning was done, Lobster Lou would grin a satisfied grin. Then he would eat a quiet dinner all alone in the tidy little kitchen.

How did Edith change after Lou gave her a job? (She started to smile and she made friends.)
I think it made Lou feel good to help Edith.

One day, a school of salmon entered the cafe. The fish were on their way back to the place they were born. They had traveled many miles that day. Lou's antennae began twitching.

Show me your antennae twitching. Now put your antennae down.
When Lou's antennae twitched, it meant he was thinking about . . . (helping someone).

The salmon were an exhausted bunch. Lobster Lou began quickly pulling chairs around and pushing tables together so the salmon could sit and rest. Then Lou hurried to the kitchen and fixed his famous fry bread and Native American berry pudding—wojape.

The salmon soon perked up. Color returned to their skin, and they began talking happily about completing their long journey home. Lobster Lou just smiled and then returned to the kitchen for a quiet dinner alone.

Lobster Lou did two things to help the salmon feel better.
What were Lou's acts of kindness? (He gave the salmon a place to rest and something to eat.)

Another day, a parade of hermit crabs arrived at the cafe. They had outgrown their shells and were in search of new homes. When the little crabs entered the cafe, they had already abandoned their old shells and were clearly distraught.

The little crabs were "distraught." How do you think they felt? (Upset)

Lobster Lou's antennae began to twitch.

Show me your antennae twitching. Now put your antennae down.

Lou's antennae were twitching, just like yours. What does that mean? (He was thinking about helping someone.)

The little crabs were upset because they had no shells. What do you think Lou will do?

Lou scurried over to the little crabs. "There, there," said Lou. "Don't worry, we will find each of you a new home." Then Lou began taking the shells from the cafe walls and fitting each little hermit crab with a new shell.

For hours, you could hear Lou saying, "And this shell is just perfect for you!"

How did Lou help the little hermit crabs? (He gave them new shells.)

In their new shells, the little hermit crabs feasted on Lou's famous southern gumbo. After they ate, Edith helped the little crabs decorate their new shells with spoons, coasters, and napkins that Lou had folded into paper cranes.

Lou watched for a bit, and then he returned to the kitchen for a quiet dinner alone.

How do you think Lou felt at the end of this day?

It was this way, day after day, at the Lobster Cafe. Lobster Lou's guests came and went, but each guest left the cafe feeling special. Lou gave all his customers the gift of kindness.

Lou had a special gift just like some of the characters in other stories we've read.
What was Lou's special gift? (Kindness)

At the beginning of the story, Lobster Lou gave his gift of kindness to Edith Eel, the salmon, and the little . . . (hermit crabs).

After one particularly busy day, Edith saw a very tired-looking Lou quietly eating his dinner alone in the kitchen. Edith said to herself, "This lobster's kindness must be returned!" Then Edith began making plans.

Edith thinks that Lobster Lou's kindness should be returned.
What do you think Edith might be planning?

We'll find out when we read Chapter 2.

END OF CHAPTER 1

CHAPTER 2 INTRODUCTION

We're reading a story called *The Lobster Cafe*.

This story takes place in the Jellyfish Hotel deep at the bottom of the . . . (sea).

Who is the story about? (Lobster Lou)

In Chapter 1, we learned that Lobster Lou had a special gift—the gift of . . . (kindness).

At the beginning of the story, Lou gave his gift of kindness to Edith Eel, and to the salmon, and to the little . . . (hermit crabs).

At the end of Chapter 1, Edith Eel saw Lobster Lou eating alone in the kitchen of the Lobster Cafe, and she began making plans.

Let's find out what Edith is planning.

Chapter 2
Returning Some Kindness

The next day, Edith arrived at the hotel a little early. Instead of reporting to the cafe, Edith stopped in the lobby.

Soon Edith had gathered a roomful of jellies around her. The jellies were bobbing up and down in agreement with Edith. "Yes, yes, yes!" they agreed. "Lobster Lou's kindness should be returned."

Did the jellyfish agree that Lobster Lou's kindness should be returned? (Yes)

The jellies floated up and down the hallways of the old hotel visiting other sea creatures and echoing Edith's words, "Acts of kindness should be returned . . . acts of kindness should be returned."

At 2:30, Edith unlocked the closed cafe. In floated the jellies, in crawled the crabs, in swam the salmon and tuna. Grandmother Octopus and her grandchildren were part of the group too. Sea creatures big and small crowded into the Lobster Cafe, and everyone busily set to work.

What do you think Edith and the rest of the sea creatures are going to do?

The crabs brought new shells and decorated the walls. The seahorses polished the silver. The tuna set up their band.

<small>It sounds to me like Lobster Lou's friends are getting ready for a party. What do you think?</small>

The salmon got busy in the kitchen. Grandmother Octopus and her grandchildren sat in one of the booths, writing and coloring.

<small>What do you think the salmon are doing in the kitchen?
What do you think Grandmother Octopus and her grandchildren are making?</small>

By 3:48, everything was ready. The salmon hid behind the counter. The jellies hung like one big chandelier at the center of the room. The seahorses and crabs all scurried to find a hiding spot.

Grandmother Octopus pulled in her arms and body until no one could see her. Everyone found a place to hide, just in time.

Why do you think all the sea creatures are hiding?

I think they are having a surprise party for Lou.

So, in the middle of the story, the sea creatures got together and planned a surprise . . . (party) for Lobster Lou.

At exactly 4:00, Lobster Lou unlocked the doors of the cafe. He entered silently.

What did Lobster Lou see?

The old lobster was stunned. He looked around in wonder.

It says Lou was stunned. That means he was surprised. Why do you think he was surprised?

Lobster Lou clapped his big claws together and muttered, "Well, I'll be . . ."

At that, all the sea creatures emerged from their hiding places and exclaimed, "Surprise! Surprise!"

Everyone, stand up and say, "Surprise! Surprise!"
Please sit down.

Lobster Lou said, "What is this? It isn't my birthday."

Grandmother Octopus stepped forward and said, "Lou, you have shown great kindness to each of us, in ways big and small. We just wanted to thank you for your kindness by doing something nice for you."

Then Grandmother Octopus and her grandchildren gave Lou a book entitled, "Lobster Lou's Acts of Kindness Great & Small."

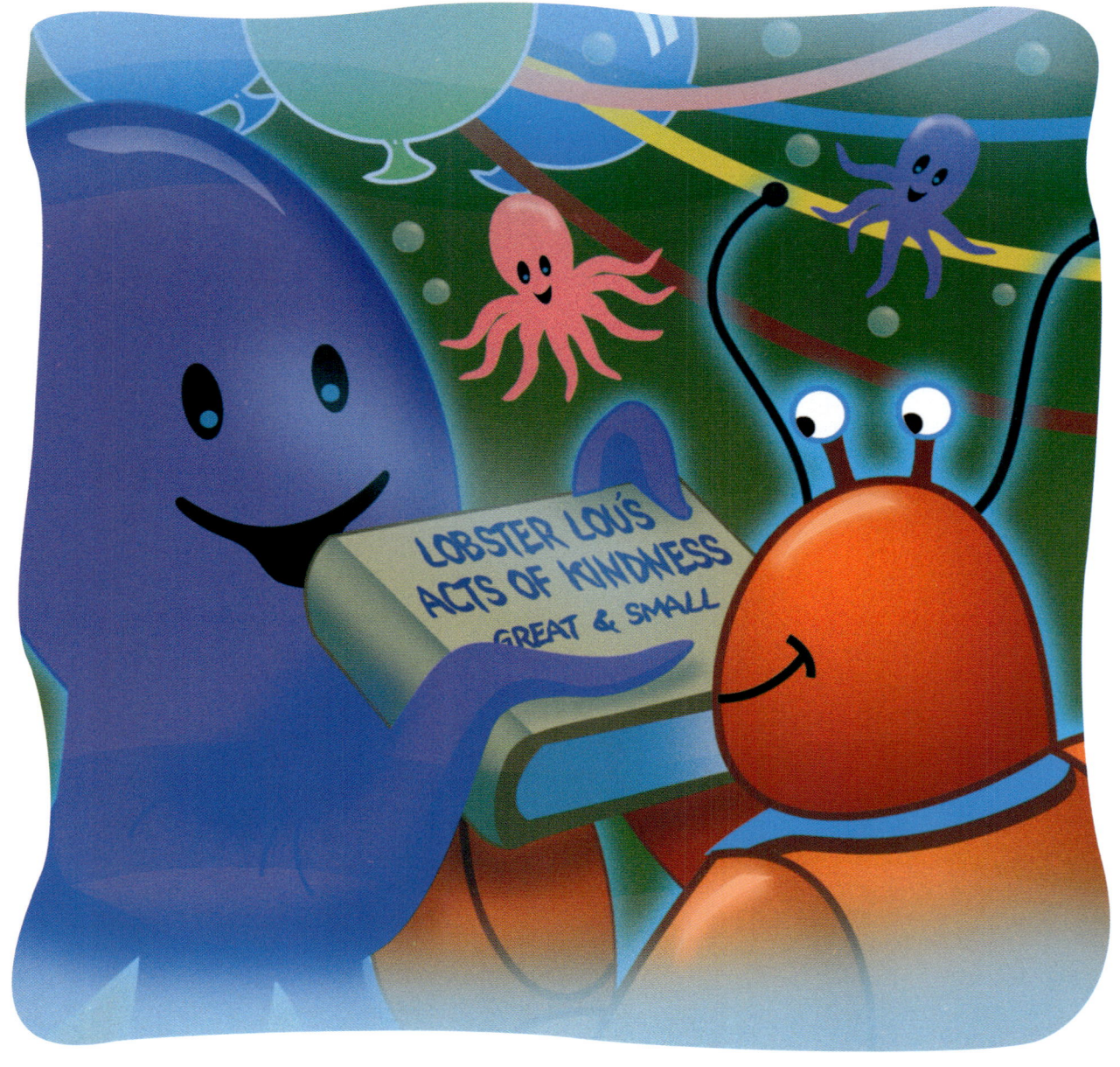

Grandmother Octopus explained why the sea creatures had the surprise party for Lou. What did she say? (They wanted to thank Lou for all the kindness he had shown to them.)
How do you think Lobster Lou felt?
I think Grandmother Octopus and her grandchildren also felt good because they had done something nice too.
What did Grandmother Octopus and her grandchildren do for Lou?

Next, the salmon talked about the great fry bread and wojape Lou had prepared for them. As the hermit crabs modeled the shells Lou had given them, the salmon brought out the special dinner they had prepared for Lou.

The evening passed quickly with laughter, music, and stories.

Towards the evening's end, the sea creatures chanted, "Speech, speech!"

Lobster Lou stood up and bowed stiffly. In his gruff old voice, Lou said, "You have honored me deeply . . . I don't know what to say." Then he said simply, "Thank you!"

Everyone, what did Lou say? (Thank you)

When Lou finished talking, Edith Eel said, "We've decided this should be Lobster Lou's Day." Everyone cheered. Then Edith pinned a beautiful heart of gold to Lou's chest. Lou smiled. Everyone smiled! It was a day to remember.

When we say that someone has a "heart of gold," it means we think that person is very kind and helpful. Why do you think Edith pinned a heart of gold on Lou's chest?

To this day, when someone needs cheering up, the sea creatures say, "Go visit Lobster Lou. He has a heart of gold."

If you were a sea creature and feeling unhappy, where would you go?
How do you think that would help?

PROCEED TO STORY SUMMARY

Story Summary

Let's retell our story.

The story takes place in the Jellyfish Hotel deep at the bottom of the . . . (sea).
Who is this story about? (Lobster Lou)
We know that Lobster Lou has the gift of . . . (kindness).

🟢 What happened at the beginning of the story? (Lobster Lou gave his gift of kindness to Edith Eel, the salmon, and the little hermit crabs.)

🟦 What happened in the middle of the story? (Edith Eel talked to the other sea creatures and together they planned a surprise party for Lobster Lou.)

27

▲
What happened at the end of the story?
(There was a surprise party for Lobster Lou
and his sea friends gave him a heart of gold.)

READER RESPONSE:

Put your arms in the air and pretend they are your antennae.

Now, think of doing something to help someone else, and then make your antennae twitch.

Put your antennae down.

Who can tell me what you would do as an act of kindness?

END OF STORY

See Teacher's Guide for related activities—Pocket Chart Retell and Bookmaking.

UNIT 23

Octopus Tales and Tentacles

Story 1 • From the Library of the Jellyfish Hotel

Story 2 • How Lucky to Be an Octopus

STORY 1 INTRODUCTION

Who remembers the story about Lobster Lou and the other sea creatures who lived in the Jellyfish Hotel?

Today we're going to read another story that takes place in the Jellyfish Hotel.

The title of this story is *From the Library of the Jellyfish Hotel.*

The story was written by Barbara Gunn and Marilyn Sprick. They are the . . . (authors).

The person who drew the pictures is Steve Clark. He is the . . . (illustrator).

From the Library of the Jellyfish Hotel

by Barbara Gunn and Marilyn Sprick
Illustrated by Steve Clark

For many years, wise old Grandmother Octopus had lived happily in the library of the sunken ship known as the Jellyfish Hotel. Over the years, she had gathered quite a collection of books.

Grandmother Octopus often would read eight books at a time! She would hold one book in each of her eight tentacles. Then she would spend all afternoon reading and thinking, reading and thinking.

Everyone, who is this story about? (Grandmother Octopus)

What do you know about Grandmother Octopus? (She is old; she is wise; she lives in the library of the sunken ship; she often reads eight books at a time.)

Grandmother Octopus loved reading to her grandchildren and the other little sea creatures when they came to visit her.

All the little sea creatures loved hearing Grandmother Octopus read *Old MacDonald's Farm* over and over and over again. They had never seen a real cow, but the little sea creatures loved singing, "With a moo moo here, and a moo moo there . . ."

Everyone, sing, "With a moo moo here, and a moo moo there . . ."

They had never seen a real pig either, but the little sea creatures loved singing, "With an oink oink here, and an oink oink there . . ."

Everyone, sing, "With an oink oink here, and an oink oink there . . ."

One day Grandmother Octopus said,
"Let's play a game called Hide 'n' Seek."

All the little sea creatures clapped.

Then Grandmother Octopus said, "While you cover your eyes and count to ten, I will hide. Then you will try to find me. I will be somewhere here in the library, but I will be very hard to find."

What game did Grandmother Octopus suggest playing? (Hide 'n' Seek)

With the wave of one of her tentacles, Grandmother Octopus jetted away. The little sea creatures covered their eyes and began to count. "One, two, three . . ."

Everyone, cover your eyes and count to ten. One, two, three, . . . ten.
Open your eyes.

At the count of ten, all the little sea creatures spread out and started looking for something that would give Grandmother Octopus away— one of her long tentacles or her large head.

What did the little sea creatures look for? (One of Grandmother Octopus's tentacles or her large head.)

A little shark looked *in* the big vase. "Not here," she said.

Where did the little shark look? (In the big vase)

The little lobster looked *under* the couch. "Not here," he bellowed.

Where did the little lobster look? (Under the couch)

The little tuna looked *on* the desk. "Not here," she announced.

Where did the little tuna look? (On the desk)

The jellies, who were bobbing around at the top of the room, looked *on top of* the chandelier. "Not here," they reported.

Where did the little jellies look? (On top of the chandelier)

The little sea creatures looked high and low. They looked in things. They looked on things. They looked under things. They looked on top of things.

Finally they gathered in the middle of the room. They were perplexed!

Perplexed is a big word that means confused. Why were the little sea creatures confused?
(They couldn't find Grandmother Octopus anywhere.)

The little shark said, "I don't get it. We've looked everywhere! Grandmother Octopus is so big, how could we have missed her? Maybe she left the library."

Where do you think Grandmother Octopus is?

Then one of the little octopuses said,
"We need to look closer. Grandmother Octopus is huge,
but like all octopuses, she is very soft and flexible.
She can squeeze into a space no bigger than a keyhole.
We need to look for her eyes.
She is watching us from somewhere in this room."

What did the little octopus tell the other little sea creatures? (Even though Grandmother Octopus was huge, she was soft and could squeeze into a little space; that they needed to look for her eyes.)

The little sea creatures started looking again. This time they looked in small places and they looked for Grandmother Octopus's eyes. It wasn't long before young Louie the Lobster spotted Grandmother Octopus hiding behind one of the book shelves.

All the little sea creatures started clapping. From that day on, "Hide 'n' Seek" was one of their favorite games.

Look at the picture. Can you see Grandmother Octopus in her hiding place?

PROCEED TO STORY SUMMARY

Story Summary

Let's retell our story.

This story takes place in the library of the Jellyfish Hotel at the bottom of the deep . . . (sea).

Who is the story about? (Grandmother Octopus and the little sea creatures)

● What happened at the beginning of the story? (Grandmother Octopus suggested that they all play Hide 'n' Seek.)

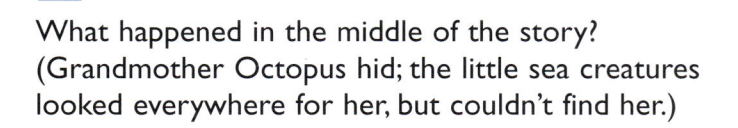

■ What happened in the middle of the story? (Grandmother Octopus hid; the little sea creatures looked everywhere for her, but couldn't find her.)

▲

What happened at the end of the story? (The little sea creatures started looking for Grandmother Octopus's eyes; Louie the Lobster finally found her hiding behind one of the bookshelves.)

READER RESPONSE:

Hide 'n' Seek became one of the little sea creatures' favorite games.

What are some of your favorite games?

END OF STORY 1

STORY 2 INTRODUCTION

In today's story, Grandmother Octopus decides it is time for the little octopuses to learn more about themselves.

The story is called *How Lucky to Be an Octopus*. What is the title? (*How Lucky to Be an Octopus*)

The author of the story is Marilyn Sprick.
Who wrote the story? (Marilyn Sprick)

The illustrator is Steve Clark.

How Lucky To Be an Octopus

by Marilyn Sprick
Illustrated by Steve Clark

One day, when the little octopuses had come to visit, Grandmother Octopus decided to play a guessing game with them.

She began, "How lucky we are to be octopuses! Just think about all the things we can do."

The little octopuses listened carefully, and then they touched their heads with the ends of their arms— to show Grandmother Octopus that they were thinking.

Everyone, show me what the little octopuses did to show Grandmother Octopus that they were thinking. That's great. Now put your hands down.

Grandmother Octopus said, "You are very smart.
Did you know that not all sea creatures are as smart as we are?"

Grandmother pointed to some of the ever-present jellies that were hanging around the library. "Our beautiful jellies have no brain at all," she said. "We octopuses, however, have a wonderful brain."

The little octopuses smiled.
They were lucky—it was a gift to be able to think.

How did the little octopuses feel about having a brain? (They thought they were lucky; it was a gift to be able to think.)

Grandmother Octopus said,
"Let's play a guessing game. It will make you use your brain!"

The little octopuses clapped with all eight of their tentacles.

Grandmother Octopus said, "I'm thinking of something we are lucky to have. Here's the first clue. It's something an octopus has that very few other animals have. What am I thinking of?"

Grandmother Octopus said she was thinking of something an octopus has.
Is it something a lot of other animals have? (No)

The little octopuses looked puzzled, so Grandmother said, "I'll give you another clue. It is something we octopuses use to catch our food."

Grandmother Octopus said she was thinking of something that octopuses use to catch their . . . (food). Can you guess what Grandmother Octopus was thinking of?

Oliver Octopus asked, "Is it our mouth?"

"That's a good guess, Oliver," said Grandmother Octopus. "We *do* use our mouths to hold our food. But I am thinking of something that whales don't have and turtles don't have. What am I thinking of?"

What do you think Grandmother Octopus is thinking about? It's something octopuses use to hold their food AND it's something most other animals don't have.

47

The little octopuses whispered together for a while, and then Oliver said, "We know. You are thinking of our *tentacles*."

Grandmother Octopus said, "Let's see if you are right.
Do whales have tentacles?"

What do you think the octopuses answered? (No)

The little octopuses giggled and said, "No!"

"Do turtles have tentacles?" asked Grandmother Octopus.

What do you think the octopuses answered? (No)

The little octopuses laughed again and said, "No!"

"Do we catch food with our tentacles?" asked Grandmother Octopus.

What do you think the octopuses answered? (Yes)

Grandmother Octopus said,
"You are right! I was thinking of our tentacles."

Then Grandmother Octopus asked, "How many tentacles do we have?"

What do you think the little octopuses said? (eight)
Let's count Grandmother Octopus's tentacles.

The little octopuses counted their tentacles.
"Eight," they announced. "We have eight tentacles."

Grandmother Octopus said, "Yes, eight tentacles . . .
the better to catch our food with!"

Grandmother Octopus said, "Now I am thinking of things we have that are round. What am I thinking of?"

Grandmother Octopus said she was thinking of things that octopuses have that are . . . (round).
Can you guess what Grandmother Octopus was thinking of?

Ozzie Octopus said, "Our eyes! Our eyes are round. Are you thinking of our eyes?"

Grandmother Octopus said, "Well, our eyes are round, but that's not what I'm thinking of. I have 240 of the round things I'm thinking of."

The little octopuses looked surprised. 240!
What did Grandmother Octopus have 240 of?

She, like all octopuses, had only two eyes.

The little octopuses talked among themselves for a while.

Then Octavia said, "We know! You are thinking of our suckers."

"Let's see," said Grandmother Octopus. "Are our suckers round?"

Onita said, "Yes."

"Do you think I have 240 of them?"

The little octopuses thought about the many suckers on Grandmother Octopus's tentacles and said, "Oh yes!"

Grandmother Octopus said, "We are very lucky! We have all those little suckers . . . the better to catch and hold our food with."

The little octopuses nodded in agreement—they were very lucky.

What do octopuses use their suckers for? (To catch and hold their food)

Finally, Grandmother Octopus said, "Now I'm thinking of something we can *do* that most animals can't do. What am I thinking of?"

Grandmother Octopus said she was thinking of something that octopuses can do—something that most other animals . . . (can't do.)

What do you think that might be?

"We eat," said Octavia, "but other animals eat, so it can't be that."

Oliver said, "We can hide under rocks, but so can other animals."

"We can change color," said Ozzie, "but there are other animals that can change color."

Grandmother Octopus said, "Ah, but you are getting closer."

Onita said, "I know, I know. We can change shape.
Is that what you were thinking of?"

Grandmother Octopus said, "Yes! You guessed it!"

What had Grandmother Octopus been thinking of? (Changing shape)

Then Grandmother said, "Octopuses are SO lucky!
Most animals can't change shape.
A turtle is always the same shape."

Oliver said, "A dolphin is always the same shape."

Ozzie said, "Lobster Lou is always the same shape."

Grandmother Octopus said, "I like the way you are using your brains!"

Do you think the little octopuses feel lucky to be able to change shape?

Grandmother said, "Our body is soft and flexible.
We are wonderful shape-shifters. We can squeeze our soft bodies into any shape we want . . . the better to hide with."

The little octopuses giggled and began pushing their flexible little bodies into funny shapes.

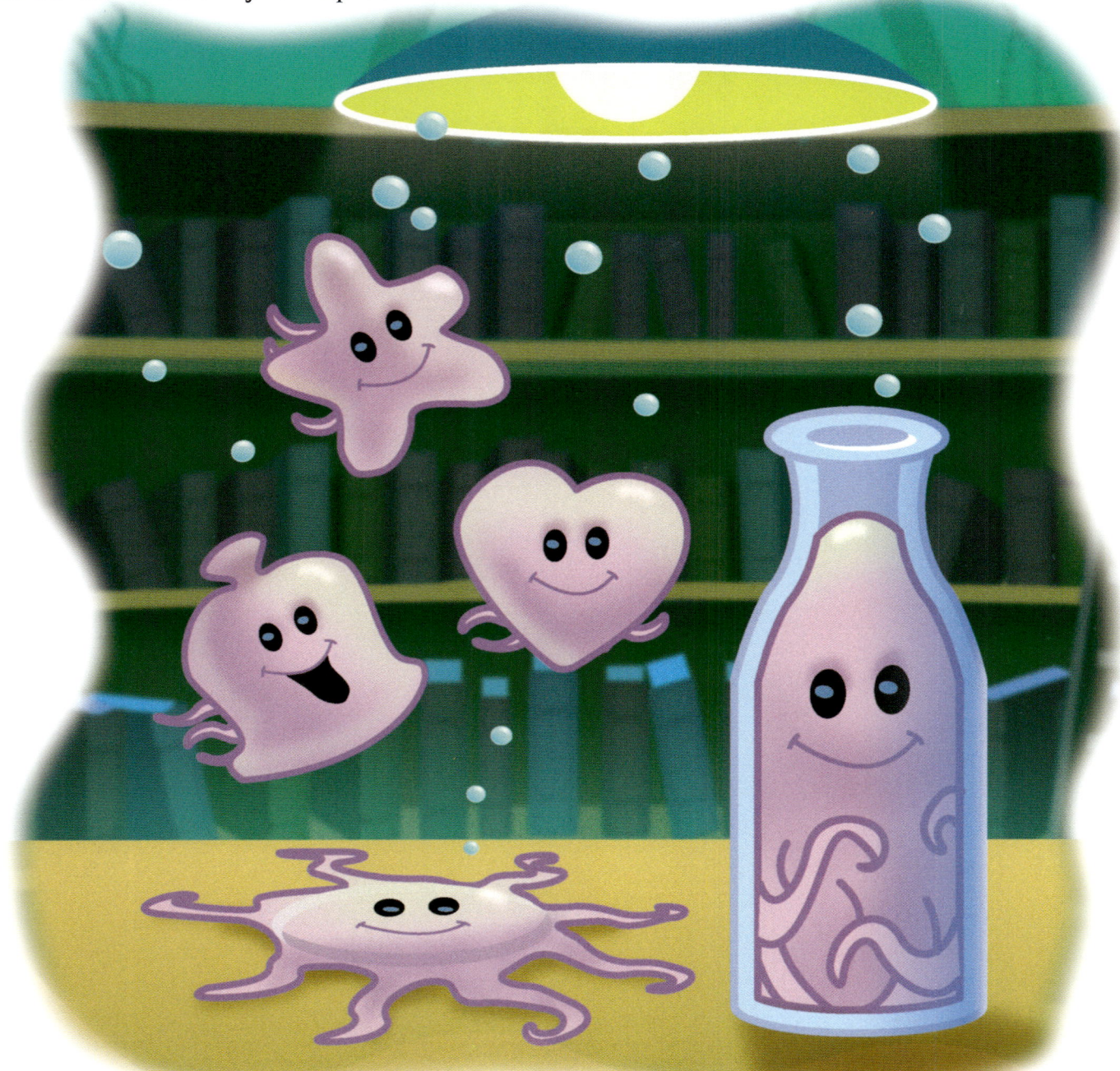

"Watch," said Oliver, and he squeezed himself into an empty water bottle that was sitting on the library table.

Everyone, see how small you can make yourself.
Do you think you could squeeze into a water bottle?

Then Grandmother Octopus said,
"Who would like to play Hide 'n' Seek?"

The little octopuses all clapped their tentacles—
they loved playing Hide 'n' Seek.

Octavia said, "We are the luckiest little octopuses in the world!"

The title of this story is *How Lucky to Be an Octopus*.
What are some of the reasons it might be lucky to be an octopus?

END OF STORY 2

See Teacher's Guide for related activity—Bookmaking.

UNIT 24

Living by the Sea

Story 1 • Malia at the Beach

Story 2 • Malia's Quilt

STORY 1 INTRODUCTION

The title of this story is *Malia at the Beach*.

Everyone, what is the title of the story? (*Malia at the Beach*)

The story is by Marilyn Sprick and Barbara Gunn. Who are the authors? (Marilyn Sprick and Barbara Gunn)

The illustrator, or person who drew the pictures, is Susan Jerde.

This story is about a girl named Malia who has a very special family and a very special grandmother.

Malia at the Beach

by Marilyn Sprick and Barbara Gunn
Illustrated by Susan Jerde

This is Malia.

She lives in a small apartment
with her mother, father, and her pet goldfish.

Everyone, who is this story about? (Malia)

Malia lives on the big island in Hawaii.
She lives in Hilo—where the air is warm and wet.
The island, like all islands, is surrounded by the sea.

Malia's family gathers at the beach for special occasions.
This is Malia's family—her mother, father, aunties, uncles, and cousins.
Next to Malia is Tūtū—Malia's grandmother.

Can you find Malia?
Who is she standing next to? (Her grandmother)
Tūtū is the Hawaiian word for grandmother. Do you have a special name for your grandmother?

Malia is jumping the little waves as they wash up onto the hard sand.

Tūtū watches and begins counting and clapping with Malia. "1, 2, 3, 4 …"

Malia jumps, and jumps, and jumps.

Everyone, stand up. Let's pretend we are jumping ten small waves.
Let's count and clap. (1, 2, 3 . . .)
Please sit down.

Malia is still jumping. Tūtū is still counting, "… 98, 99, 100, 101 …"

Let's count with Tūtū starting at 102. (102, 103, 104, 105, 106, 107, 108, 109)
Let's stop and see what Tūtū says.

At 109, Tūtū laughs and says, "Malia … the waves have been coming since I was born, and my mother before me. I think you had better stop."

Malia is tired, so she stops jumping and sits in the warm dry sand with Tūtū.
"What shall we count now, Tūtū?"

Tūtū looks around. "We can count the birds in the sky."

Malia looks up and giggles. "That's too easy, Tūtū.
There are only three birds in the sky."

Tūtū smiles and winks at Malia. Malia is getting too smart to trick.

Everyone, show me what Tūtū did.

Yes, Tūtū winked to show Malia that she was just kidding.

Malia says, "Tūtū, let's count the grains of sand on the beach."

Tūtū and Malia look up and down the beach at all the grains of sand.

Then Malia laughs and winks at Tūtū. Tūtū is too smart to trick.

Everyone, show me what Malia did.

Yes, Malia winked at Tūtū to show her that she was just . . . (kidding).

See Malia climbing in the rocks with her cousins. Listen.

> One little, two little, three opihi;
>
> four little, five little, six opihi;
>
> seven little, eight little, nine opihi;
>
> ten opihi for my lunch.

Malia is singing her counting song.

Everyone, let's sing Malia's opihi counting song. (One little, two little, three opihi; four little, five little, six opihi; seven little, eight little, nine opihi; ten opihi for my lunch!)

Malia's aunties and uncles shuck the opihi from their shells with a spoon. Then the opihi are salted and put in a bowl. The opihi will be a special treat.

Opihi are kind of like clams. They are a special Hawaiian treat. Does your family have a special food?

After eating, there is much talk and laughter.

Then Malia sees one of her aunties light the candles.

One, two, three, four, five, six, seven … seven candles.

Malia is lifted to a cousin's shoulders, and everyone sings "Happy Birthday" to Malia.

The special occasion is Malia's birthday.

Malia's family gathers at the beach for special occasions. What is today's special occasion? (Malia's birthday)
Everyone, let's sing "Happy Birthday" to Malia. (Happy Birthday to . . .)

It has been a good day.

As the grown-ups pack up,
Malia and Tūtū sit in the sand and
watch the sun as it steps from the sky into the ocean.

I liked this story because it reminds me of my family.
Who liked this story? Why?

END OF STORY 1

STORY 2 INTRODUCTION

Last time, we read a story about a Hawaiian girl named Malia.
Malia was seven in that story.
Today we're going to read another story about Malia.
The story is called *Malia's Quilt*.
In this story, we go back to a time when Malia was younger.
Marilyn Sprick and Barbara Gunn are the authors of the story.
Susan Jerde is the illustrator.

Malia's Quilt

by Marilyn Sprick and Barbara Gunn
Illustrated by Susan Jerde

One day, when Malia was five, her mother said,
"Malia, Tūtū isn't well, so she is going to come live with us."

Malia thought of her grandmother's laugh and she smiled.

Have you ever had a relative move in with your family?

72

That night, Malia's mother and father brought another bed into Malia's small bedroom. The dresser, and Malia's goldfish, were moved into the hallway.

Why did they move Malia's dresser to the hallway? (To make room for the bed for Tūtū)

73

Tūtū arrived the next day.
She was very quiet.
This made Malia sad.

Show me how Malia felt.
Yes, Malia was sad because her grandmother was sick.

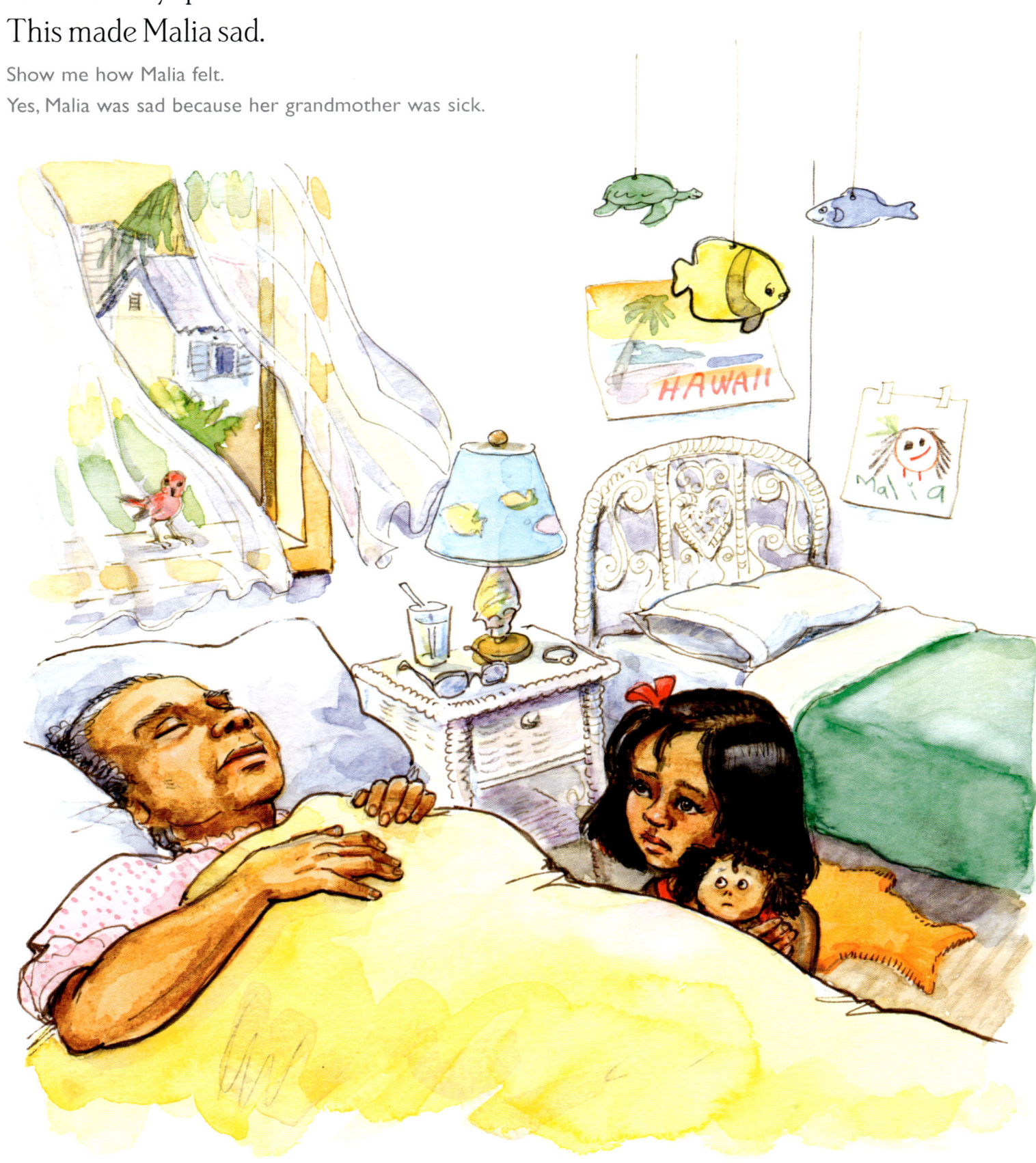

Tūtū slept all day and all night for many days.
Malia's mother told her, "Tūtū is very tired."

Slowly Tūtū's smile started to come back. Then one day, when Malia got home from school, she heard Tūtū's gentle laugh. Tūtū was on the lanai watching a small bird. This made Malia happy.

Why was Malia happy? (Because she heard Tūtū laugh)
Yes, she was happy because Tūtū was feeling better.

Not long after that, Tūtū began making a quilt.

She stood at the kitchen table. Snip, snip, snip.

Then Tūtū and Malia's mother stretched a big piece of white cloth across a quilting frame in the living room. The little apartment got even smaller!

What is Malia's grandmother making? (A quilt)

Sometimes, Malia and her friends would play under the quilting frame.
It made a perfect tent.

Raise your hand if you've ever played in a tent?

Day after day, Tūtū stitched. Stitch, stitch, stitch.

Everyday after school, Malia would ask, "How many stitches did you make today?"

Then Malia would sing her counting song.

>One little, two little, three little stitches;
>
>four little, five little, six little stitches;
>
>seven little, eight little, nine little stitches;
>
>ten little stitches in the quilt.

Everyone, let's sing Malia's stitching song. (One little, two little, three little stitches . . .)

Some days when Malia asked, "How many stitches today, Tūtū?"
Malia and her grandmother would look at the quilt and together say,
"Many! Too many to count!"
Then they would laugh.

Gradually, the little smile wrinkles around Tūtū's eyes came back. Malia could tell that her grandmother felt better. She laughed when the wind made coconuts fall from the trees, and she laughed when Malia gave her a hug.

How could Malia tell that Tūtū was feeling better? (Tūtū laughed more; the little smile wrinkles around Tūtū's eyes came back.)

Everyday there were more stitches in the quilt—hundreds and hundreds of stitches!

Then, one day, the quilt was done!

Malia thought it was the most beautiful thing she had ever seen. Tūtū just smiled.

They carefully folded the quilt and put it at the end of Tūtū's bed.

What did Malia think about Tūtū's quilt? (It was the most beautiful thing she had ever seen.)

Not long after that, Uncle Kai came to get Tūtū.
It was time for Tūtū to go home. Tūtū hugged Malia goodbye.

How do you think Malia is feeling now?

Malia sat quietly on her bed that night. Something didn't feel right. The room felt empty.

Malia's mother came in and sat down next to her. She had a package wrapped in brown paper. Malia's mother said, "Tūtū left something for you."

Malia pulled the string that was around the package. The brown paper fell open.

What do you think is in the package?

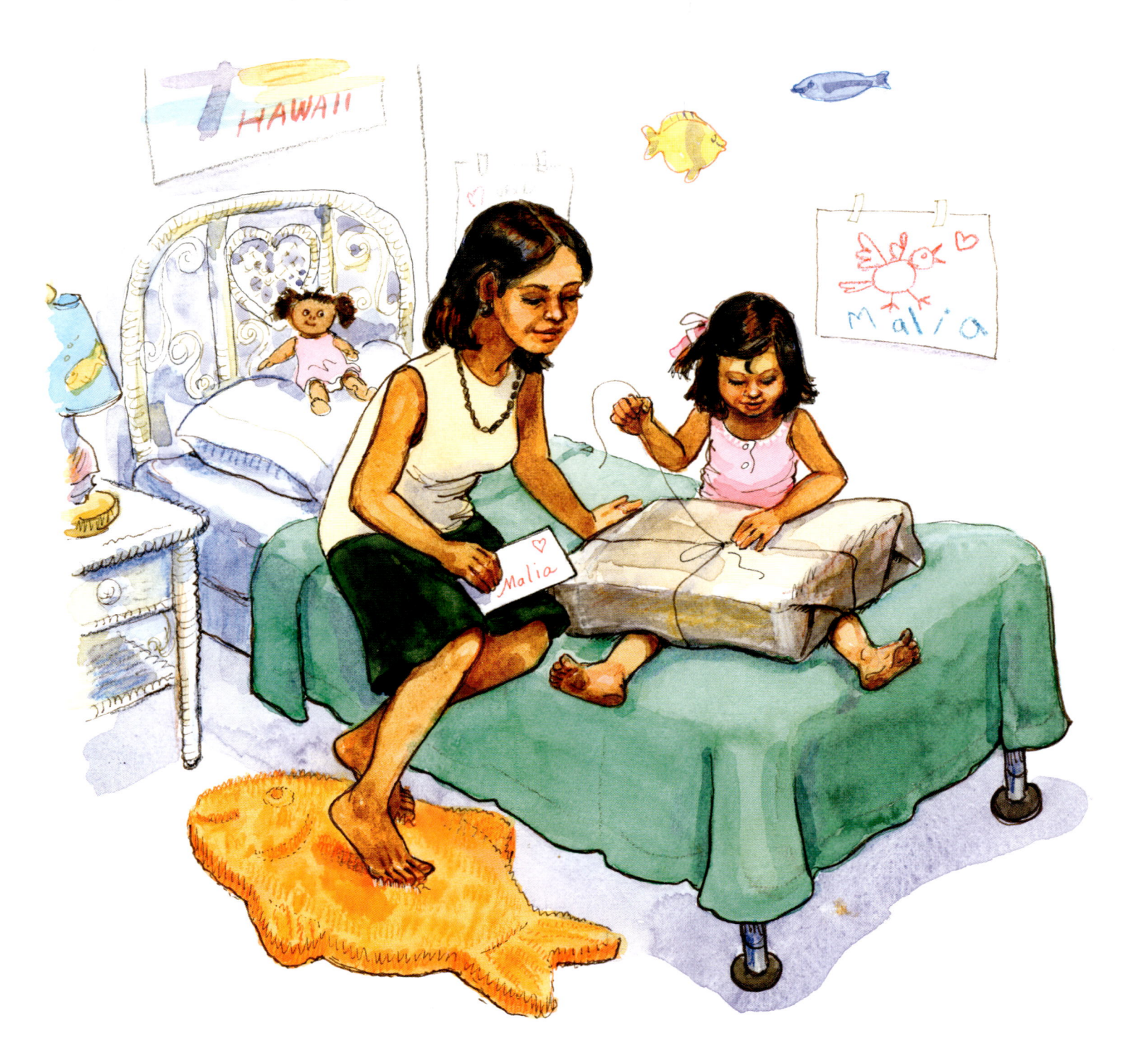

It was the quilt! Malia hugged the beautiful quilt.

Her mother said, "There's a note, Malia. I will read it to you."

Dear Malia—

*This quilt will keep your room full of love.
Remember, I will see you on Saturday.*

Mahalo,

Tūtū

That night Malia dreamed of hunting for opihi on the beach while Tūtū watched and smiled.

Malia got a very special gift from her grandmother. Have you ever gotten a special gift from someone?

END OF STORY 2

See Teacher's Guide for related activities: Pocket Chart Retell and Bookmaking.

84

Mrs. B is a teacher at the Ant School in the *Read Well K* stories. She is featured throughout the program, and is also the acronym for the author of many of the stories in *Read Well K*. When program authors found that shared story writing allowed them to combine their talents, Mrs. B was the designated author. Mrs. B stands for Marilyn, Richard, Shelley, and Barbara.

M is for Marilyn Sprick.

Marilyn Maeda Sprick is a third generation Japanese American. She and her husband, Randy, have two grown children. They live in the woods near Eugene, Oregon, with their two dogs. Marilyn has always loved writing and art, but most of all she loves teaching children of all ages how to read well.

R is for Richard Dunn.

Richard Dunn is a kindergarten teacher in Seattle, Washington. He lives with his wife, two children, and a big white cat. During his free time, Richard loves to play with his children, read, and spend time outdoors hiking and camping.

S is for Shelley V. Jones.

Shelley V. Jones teaches in Oregon and lives with her husband and a beagle named Macintosh. She is a mom with two grown kids. Shelley loves books and music, and has spent her life teaching reading and music to people of all ages.

B is for Barbara Gunn.

Barbara Gunn grew up in California, where she spent her summers swimming, bike riding, and making up stories. Now she lives in Eugene, Oregon, with her husband, Steve, and two cats, Oreo and Tillie. Barbara has two grown children. She still likes making up stories, and especially enjoys researching how to teach children to read well.

Steve Clark lives in Loveland, Colorado with his lovely wife, beautiful little daughter, big slobbery dog, and unpredictable cat. He enjoys doing his artwork late at night when the refrigerator is left unguarded and the world seems just a little bit more mysterious.

Susan Jerde lives in Eugene, Oregon with her husband, a dog, two cats, and two fishponds. She has a daughter away at college. She has loved to draw since she was a little girl, especially animals. When she isn't drawing pictures she likes to ride horses and go camping with her family. Susan also grows lots of fruits, vegetables and flowers in her garden.

Read Well